MEMORY GARDENS

Also by Robert Creeley

Robert Creeley
MEMORY GARDENS

Well, while I'm here I'll
            do the work —
and what's the work?
            To ease the pain of living.
Everything else, drunken
            dumbshow.

— Allen Ginsberg, "Memory Gardens"

A NEW DIRECTIONS BOOK

ACKNOWLEDGMENTS

Grateful acknowledgment is made to the editors and publishers of magazines, chapbooks, broadsides, and anthologies in which many of the poems in this collection first appeared. Magazines: *Columbia, Continental Drifter, Epoch, Slow Mountain, St. Mark's Poetry Project Newsletter.* Chapbooks. *A Calendar* (The Toothpaste Press, 1983), *Four Poems* (Handmade Books, 1984), *Jim Dine: Five Themes* (Walker Art Center, Minneapolis, 1984), *Memories* (Pig Press, 1984). Broadsides: "Bookcase" (The Folger Library, 1982), "Hotel Schrieber, Heidelberg" (The Toothpaste Press, for the Walker Art Center, 1984), "Wyatt's May" (The Toothpaste Press, 1983). Anthologies: *Peace or Perish: A Crisis Anthology* (Poets for Peace, 1983), *In Celebration: Anemos,* Festschrift for Denise Levertov (Matrix Press, 1983).

The epigraph on the title page is quoted from Allen Ginsberg's *The Fall of America: Poems of These States 1965–1971*, Pocket Poets Series #30, Copyright © 1972 by City Lights Books.

The epigraph on page 47 is quoted from Charles Olson's *Maximus Poems,* Copyright © 1983 by the Regents of the University of California; used by permission of the University of California Press.

"Après Anders," the sequence on pages 42–44, is an improvisation on poems by Richard Anders found in his collection *Preussische zimmer* (1975).

Manufactured in the United States of America
First published clothbound and as New Directions Paperbook 613 in 1986
Published simultaneously in Canada by Penguin Books Canada Limited

Library of Congress Cataloging-in-Publication Data
Creeley, Robert, 1926–
  Memory gardens.
  (A New Directions Book)
  I. Title.
PS3505.R43M43 1986   811'.54   85-29723
ISBN 0-8112-0973-3
ISBN 0-8112-0974-1 (pbk.)

New Directions Books are published for James Laughlin
by New Directions Publishing Corporation,
80 Eighth Avenue, New York 10011

For Penelope, Willy, and Hannah

I

HEAVEN KNOWS

Seemingly never until one's dead
is there possible measure—

but of what then or for what
other than the same plagues

attended the living with misunderstanding
and wanted a compromise as pledge

one could care for any of them
heaven knows, if that's where one goes.

FORTY

The forthright, good-natured faith
of man hung on crane up

forty stories with roof scaffolding
burning below him forty feet,

good warm face, black hair,
confidence. He said, when

the firemen appeared, he said
I'm glad to see you,

glad not to be there alone.
How old? Thirty, thirty-five?

He has friends to believe in,
those who love him.

OUT

Within pitiless
indifference
things left
out.

NEW ENGLAND

Work, Christian, work!
Love's labors before you go
carrying lights like the
stars are all out and
tonight is the night.

TOO LATE

You tried to answer the questions attractively,
your name, your particular interests,

what you hoped life would prove,
what you owned and had with you,

your so-called billfold an umbilical,
useless, to the sack you'd carried

all your sad life, all your vulnerability,
but couldn't hide, couldn't now say,

brown hair, brown eyes, steady,
I think I love you.

ROOM

Quick stutters of incidental
passage going back

and forth, quick
breaks of pattern, slices

of the meat, two
rotten tomatoes, an incidental

snowstorm, death, a girl
that looks like you later

than these leaves of
grass, trees, birds, under

water, empty passage-
way, and no way back.

HOTEL

It isn't in the world of
fragile relationships

or memories, nothing
you could have brought with you.

It's snowing in Toronto.
It's four-thirty, a winter evening,

and the tv looks like a faded
hailstorm. The people

you know are down the hall,
maybe, but you're tired,

you're alone, and that's happy.
Give up and lie down.

ECHO

Pushing out from
this insistent

time makes
all of it

empty, again
memory.

EARTH

And as the world is flat or round
out over those difficult dispositions

of actual water, actual earth,
each thing invariable, specific,

I think no rock's hardness,
call on none to gainsay me,

be only here as and forever
each and every thing is.

DOGS

I've trained them
to come,

to go away again,
to sit, to stand,

to wait
on command,

or I'd like to
be the master who

tells them all
they can't do.

VISION

Think of the size of it,
so big, if you could remember
what it was or where.

RELIGION

Gods one would have
hauled out like props
to shore up the invented
inside-out proposals

of worlds equally like shams
back of a shabby curtain
only let in the duped,
the dumbly despairing.

So flutter the dead
back of the scene
and along with them
the possibly still living.

THE ROCK

Shaking hands again
from place of age,
out to the one

is walking down
the garden path
to be as all reunited.

THANKSGIVING'S DONE

All leaves gone, yellow
light with low sun,

branches edged
in sharpened outline

against far-up pale sky.
Nights with their blackness

and myriad stars, colder
now as these days go by.

GO

Push that little
thing up and the
other right down.
It'll work.

MAIN AND MERRIMAC

"It just plain
hurts to work—"
Christ holds
up hands in
mock despair
concrete bright
sun with faint
first green of
leaves this morn-
ing's gone to
spring's first day.

FOR PEN

Lady moon
light white
flowers open
in sweet silence.

FOR J.D.

Seeing is believing—
times such things
alter all one
had known.

These times, places,
old, echoing
clothes, hands—tools,
almost walking.

Your heart *as big as all outdoors* . . .
where tree grows,
gate was
waiting.

ALWAYS

Sweet sister Mary's gone
away. Time fades on and on.

The morning was so bright, so clear
blurs in the eye, fades also.

Time tells what after all.
It's always now, always here.

EDGE

Edge of place
put on between

its proposed
place in

time
and space.

MASSACHUSETTS MAY

Month one was born in
particular emphasis
as year comes round
again. Laconic, diverse

sweet May of my boyhood,
as the Memorial Day Parade
marches through those memories.
Or else the hum and laze

of summer's sweet patterns,
dragonflies, grasshoppers,
ladyslippers, and ponds—
School's end. Summer's song.

MEMORIES

Hello, duck,
in yellow

cloth stuffed from
inside out,

little
pillow.

ECHO

Back in time
for supper
when the lights

II

WALL

I've looked at this wall
for months, bricks
faded, chipped, edge of roof

fixed with icicles
like teeth,
arch of window

opposite, blistered
white paint, a trim
of grey blue.

Specific limit—
of what? A shell
of house, no one's home,

tenuous,
damp emptiness
under a leaky roof.

Careless of what else,
wall so close,
insistent,

to my own—
can push
with eye, thinking

where one can't go,
those crushed
in so-called blackness,

despair. This easy
admission's
no place walls

can echo,
real or unreal.
They sit between

inside and out—
like in school, years ago,
we saw *Wall,* heard

Wall say, "Thus have I,
Wall, my part discharged so;/
And, being done,

thus Wall away doth go"—
Clouds overhead, patch of
shifting blue sky. Faint sun.

I'LL WIN

I'll win the way
I always do
by being gone
when they come.

When they look, they'll see
nothing of me
and where I am
they'll not know.

This, I thought, is my way
and right or wrong
it's me. Being dead, then,
I'll have won completely.

EATS

Self-shrinking focus
mode of deployment
of people met in casual
engagement, social—

Not the man I am
or even was, have constructed
some pattern, place
will be as all.

Bored, shrink into
isolated fading
out of gross, comfortable
contact, hence *out to lunch.*

FOR THE NEW YEAR

Rid forever of *them* and *me,*
the ridiculous small places
of the patient hates, the meager

agreement of unequal people—
at last all subject to
hunger, despair, a common grief.

BOOKCASE

One cannot offer
to emptiness

more than regret. The persons
no longer are there,

their presence become
a resonance, something

inside. Postcard—
"still more to have . . .

"of talking to you"—
found in book

in this chaos—
dead five years.

BABY DISASTER

Blurred headlights of the cars out there
war of the worlds or something,
ideas of it all like dropped change,
trying to find it on the sidewalk at night.

Nothing doing anymore, grown up, moved out,
piddling little's going to come of it,
all you put in the bank or spent
you didn't want to, wanted to keep it all.

Walk on by, baby disaster.
Sad for us all finally, totally,
going down like in Sargasso Sea
of everything we ever thought to.

SOUND

Shuddering racket of
air conditioner's colder

than imagined winter,
standing lonely,

constancy's not
only love's,

not such faith
in mere faithfulness—

sullen sound.

FOR J.D. (2)

Pass on by, love,
wait by that garden gate.
Swing on, up
on heaven's gate.

The confounding, confronted
pictures of world
brought to signs
of its insistent self

are here in all colors, sizes—
a heart as big as all outdoors,
a weather of spaces,
intervals between silences.

PICTURE

for D.L.

Great giggles,
chunky lumps,
packed flesh,
good nature—

like an apple,
a pear, an immaculate
strawberry, a
particular pomegranate.

And that's the way you saw me, love?
Just so.
Was there nothing else struck you?
No.

FOUR FOR JOHN DALEY

MOTHER'S THINGS

I wanted approval,
carrying with me
things of my mother's
beyond their use to me—

worn-out clock,
her small green lock box,
father's engraved brass plate
for printing calling cards—

such size of her still
calls out to me
with that silently
expressive will.

ECHO

Lonely in
no one
to hold it with—

the responsible
caring
for those one's known.

LEAVING

My eye teared,
lump in throat—
I was going
away from here

and everything that
had come with me
first was waiting
again to be taken.

All the times
I'd looked, held,
handled that or this
reminded me

no fairness, justice,
in life, not
that can stand
with those abandoned.

BUFFALO AFTERNOON

Greyed board fence
past brown open door,
overhead weather's
early summer's.

The chairs sit various,
what's left, the
emptiness, this
curious waiting to go.

I look up to eyes
of Willy's battered
plastic horse, a dog
for its face.

All here,
even in the absence
as if all were
so placed in vacant space.

FORT WILLIAM HENRY / PEMAQUID

Squat round stone tower
o'erlooks the quiet water.

Might in olden days here
had literally accomplished power

as they must have hauled the rocks
from the coves adjacent

to defend their rights
in this abstract place

of mind and far waters
they'd come all the way over

to where presently small son paddles,
flops on bottom in sea's puddle.

NOTHING

Ant pushes across rock face.
No sign of age there

nor in the outstretched water
looks like forever.

Dried seaweed, this ground-down sand,
or the sky where sun's reached peak

and day moves to end—
still nothing done, enough said.

FOR TED BERRIGAN

After, size of place
you'd filled
in suddenly emptied
world all too apparent

and as if New England
shrank, grew physically
smaller like Connecticut,
Vermont—all the little

things otherwise unattended
so made real by you,
things to do today,
left empty, waiting

sadly for no one
will come again now.
It's all moved inside,
all that dear world

in mind for forever,
as long as one walks
and talks here,
thinking of you.

HOTEL SCHRIEDER, HEIDELBERG

Offed tv screen's
reflection room
across with gauze
draped window see
silent weeping face
Marcel Marceau from
balcony seat was memory's
Paris early fifties how
was where and when
with whom we
sat there, watching?

"ICH BIN . . ."

Ich Bin
2 *Öl*-tank

yellow squat
by railroad

shed train's
zapped past

round peculiar
empty small

town's ownership
fields' flat

production towered
by obsolescent hill-

side memory echoing
old worn-out castle.

APRÈS ANDERS

HAHA

In her hair the
moon, with
the moon, wakes water—

balloon hauls her
into the blue. She

fängt, she
in the woods
faints, finds, fakes

fire, high in
Erlen, oil, Earl—

like a *Luftschiffern,*
tails of high clouds up
there, one says.

KAPUT KASPER'S LATE LOVE

I was
"kaput Kasper"
in *Fensterfrost,*

window shade auntie,
mother's faltering bundle.
Blood flecks on some
wind flint horizon.

I knew my swollen loaf,
Lauf, like, out, *aus*
es floats, it *flötete.*

Sie sagte, said
the night stuck
two eyes in her heart (head).

I *griff,* grabbed, griped,
in the empty holes, held
on to holes

unter der Stirn,
under stars, the stars
in the sky tonight.

DEN ALTEN

Then to old Uncle Emil
den du immer mimst
you always

missed,
missed most,
häng einem alten Haus

in fear, hung
from a rafter, a
beam old

Uncle Emil you
immer mimst
over the logical river

Fluss in the
truly really
feuchten clay, fucked finished clay.

LATE LOVE

Stuck in her stone hut
he fights to get the window up.

Her loopy Dachshunds
have made off with the pupils

of his eyes, like, or else
now from summit to summit

of whatever mountains against which
he thinks he hears the stars crash,

sounds truly *nada*
in all the sad façade.

AGAIN

The woman who
came out of the shadow

of the trees asked
after a time "what time is it"

her face
for a second

in my head
was there again

and I felt again
as against this emptiness

where also
I'd been.

WAITING

Waiting for the object,
the abject adjunct—

the loss of feel here,
field, faded.

Singing inside,
outside grey, wet,

cold out. The weather
doesn't know it,

goes only on to
wherever.

HANDS

Reaching out to shake,
take, the hand,

hands, take in
hand hands.

". . . come, poppy, when will you bloom?"

—Charles Olson

FATHERS

Scattered, aslant
faded faces a column
a rise of the packed
peculiar place to a
modest height makes
a view of common lots
in winter then, a ground
of battered snow crusted
at the edges under
it all, there under
my fathers their
faded women, friends,
the family all echoed,
names trees more tangible
physical place more tangible
the air of this place the road
going past to Watertown
or down to my mother's
grave, my father's grave, not
now this resonance of
each other one was his, his
survival only, his curious
reticence, his dead state,
his emptiness, his acerbic
edge cuts the hands to
hold him, hold on, wants
the ground, *wants* this frozen ground.

MEMORY GARDENS

Had gone up to
down or across dis-
placed eagerly
unwitting hoped for

mother's place in time
for supper just
to say anything
to her again one

simple clarity her
unstuck glued
deadness emptied
into vagueness hair

remembered wisp that
smile like half
her eyes brown eyes
her thinning arms

could lift her
in my arms so
hold to her so
take her in my arms.

FLICKER

In this life the
half moment
ago is just

at this edge
of curious place you
reach for feel

that instant shining
even still wet's
gone faded flashlight.

MY OWN STUFF

"My own stuff" a
flotsam I could
neither touch quite
nor get hold of, fluff,
as with feathers, milk-
weed, the evasive
lightness distracted yet
insistent to touch
it kept poking, trying
with my stiffened
fingers to get hold of
its substance I had
even made to be
there its only
reality my own.

WINDOW

The upper part is snow,
white, lower, grey
to brown, a thicket,
lacing, light seeming
hedge of branches, twigs,
growths of a tree, trees,
see eyes, holes, through
the interlacings, the white
emphatic spaced places
of the snow, the gravity,
weight, holds it, on top,
as down under, the grey,
brown, edged red, or
ground it has to come to,
must all come down.

WINTER MORNING

The sky's like a pewter
of curiously dulled blue,
and "My heart's in the highlands . . . ,"
feels the day beginning again.

And whatever, whatever, says it
again, and stays here, stays
here with its old hands,
holds on with its stiff, old fingers,

can come too, like they say,
can come with me into this patient weather,
and won't be left alone, no, never alone ever
        again,
in whatever time's left for us here.

QUESTIONS

In the photograph you felt
grey, disregarded, your head
obscured by the company
around you, presuming
some awkward question. Were you dead?

Could this self-indulgence extend
to all these others, even
persuade them to do something
about you, or *with* you, given
they had their own things to do?

LOVERS

Remember? as kids
we'd looked in crypt
had we fucked? we
walked a Saturday
in cemetery it
was free the flowers
the lanes we looked
in past the small
barred window into
dark of tomb when
it looked out at us
face we saw white
looking out at us
inside the small
room was it man
who worked there? dead
person's fraught skull?

FUNERAL

Why was grandma
stacked in sitting room
so's people could come
in, tramp through.

What did we eat
that day before
we all drove off
to the cemetery in Natick

to bury her with grandpa
back where the small air-
port plane flew over
their modest lot there

where us kids could
look through the bushes,
see plane flying around or
sitting on the ground.

SUPPER

Time's more than
twilight mother at
the kitchen table over
meal the boiled potatoes
Theresa's cooked with meat.

CLASSICAL

One sits vague in this sullenness.
Faint, greying winter, hill
with its agéd, incremental institution,
all a seeming dullness of enclosure

above the flat lake—oh youth,
oh cardboard cheerios of time,
oh helpless, hopeless faith of empty trust,
apostrophes of leaden aptitude, my simple
    children,

why not anger, an argument, a proposal,
why the use simply of all you are or might be
by whatever comes along, your persons
fixed, hung, splayed carcasses, on abstract rack?

One instant everything must always change,
your life or death, your articulate fingers lost
in meat time, head overloaded, fused circuit,
all cheap tears, regrets, permissions forever
    utterly forgot.

MOTHER'S PHOTOGRAPH

Could you see present
sad investment of
person, its clothes,
gloves and hat,

as against yourself
backed to huge pine tree,
lunch box in hand in
homemade dress aged

ten, to go to school
and learn to be somebody,
find the way will
get you out of the

small place of home
and bring them with
you, out of it too,
sit them down in a new house.

VALENTINE

Had you a dress
would cover you all
in beautiful echoes
of all the flowers I know,

could you come back again,
bones and all,
just to talk
in whatever sound,

like letters spelling words,
this one says, *Mother,*
I love you—
that one, *my son.*

LECTURE

What was to talk to,
around in half-circle,
the tiers, ledges
of their persons

attending expectation,
something's to happen,
waiting for words,
explanations—

thought of cigarette
smoke, a puff recollected,
father's odor
in bed years ago.

BACK

Suppose it all turns into, again,
just the common, the expected
people, and places, the distance
only some change and possibly one

or two among them all, gone—
that word again—or simply more
alone than either had been
when you'd first met them. But you

also are not the same,
as if whatever you were were
the memory only, your hair, say,
a style otherwise, eyes now

with glasses, clothes even
a few years can make look
out of place, or where you
live now, the phone, all of it

changed. Do you simply give
them your address? Who?
What's the face in the mirror then.
Who are you calling.

KNOCK KNOCK

Say nothing
to it.
Push it away.
Don't answer.

Be grey,
oblique presence.
Be nothing
there.

If it speaks
to you, it
only wants
you for itself

and it has
more than you,
much
more.

HEAVY

Friend's story of dead whale on California beach
which the people blow up to get rid of and for
    weeks
after they're wiping the putrescent meat off their
    feet,

like, and if that's a heavy one, consider Meese
and what it takes to get rid of mice
and lice and just the nice people next door, *oh*
    yeah . . .

SKIN AND BONES

It ain't no sin
to sit down
take off your coat
wait for whatever

happens here
whenever it happens
for whatever.
It's your own skin.

THE DOCTOR

Face of my
father looks out

from magazine's
page on back

of horse at eight
already four

more than
I was when

the doctor died
as both

mother and Theresa
used to say, "the

doctor," whose
saddened son I

was and have
to be, my sister

older speaks of
him, "He felt

that with Bob
he was starting

over, perhaps, and
resolved not

to lose this son
as he had Tom and Phil . . ."

Nothing said
to me, no words more

than echoes, a
smell I remember

of cigarette box, a
highball glass,

man in bed with
mother, the voice

lost now. "Your
father was such

a Christmas fellow!"
So happy, empty

in the leftover
remnants of whatever

it was, the doctor's
house, the doctor's family.

LOST

One could reach up into
the air, to see if it was

still there, shoved back
through the hole, the little

purpose, hidden it was,
the small, persisting agencies,

arms and legs, the ears
of wonder covered with area,

all eyes, the echoes, the aches
and pains of patience, the

inimitable here and now of all,
ever again to be one and only one,

to look back to see the long distance
or to go forward, having only lost.

OLD

Its fears are
particular, head,

hands, feet, the
toes in two

patient rows,
and what comes

now is less,
least of all it

knows, wants in
any way to know.

THERE

On such a day
did it happen

by happy coincidence
just here.

LANGUAGE

Are all your
preoccupations un-

civil, insistent
caviling, mis-

taken dis-
criminating?

DAYS

for H.H.C.

In that strange light,
garish like wet blood,

I had no expectations
or hopes, nothing any more

one shouts at life to wake it up,
be nice to us—simply scared

you'd be hurt, were already
changed. I was, your head

out, looked— I want each
day for you, each single day

for you, give them
as I can to you.

HEAVENLY HANNAH

Oh Hannie
help me
help

IV

A CALENDAR

THE DOOR

Hard to begin
always again and again,

open that door
on yet another year

faces two ways
but goes only one.

Promises, promises . . .
What stays true to us

or to the other
here waits for us.

(JANUARY)

HEARTS

No end to it if
"heart to heart"
is all there is

to buffer, put against
harshness of this weather,
small month's meagerness—

"Hearts are trumps,"
win out again
against all odds,

beat this
drab season of bitter cold
to save a world.

(FEBRUARY)

MARCH MOON

Already night and day move
more closely, shyly, under this frozen

white cover, still rigid with
locked, fixed, deadened containment.

The dog lies snuffling, snarling
at the sounds beyond the door.

She hears the night, the new moon,
the white, wan stars, the

emptiness momently will break
itself open, howling, intemperate.

(MARCH)

"WHAN THAT APRILLE . . ."

When April with his showers sweet
the drought of March has pierced to the root
and bathed every vein in such liqueur
its virtue thus becomes the flower . . .

When faded harshness moves to be
gone with such bleakness days had been,
sunk under snows had covered them,
week after week no sun to see,

then restlessness resolves in rain
after rain comes now to wash all clean
and soften buds begin to spring
from battered branches, patient earth.

Then into all comes life again,
which times before had one thought dead,
and all is outside, nothing in—
and so it once more does begin.

(APRIL)

> In May my welth and eke my liff, I say,
> have stonde so oft in such perplexitie . . .
> —Sir Thos. Wyatt

In England May's mercy
is generous. The mustard

covers fields in broad swaths,
the hedges are white flowered—

but it is meager, so said.
Having tea here, by the river,

huge castle, cathedral, time
passes by in undigested,

fond lumps. Wyatt died
while visiting friends nearby,

and is buried in Sherborne Abbey—
"England's first sonnet-maker . . ."

May May reward him and all
he stood for more happily now

because he sang May,
maybe for all of us:

"Arise, I say, do May some obseruance!
Let me in bed lie dreming in mischaunce . . ."

So does May's mind remember all
it thought of once.

(MAY)

79

SUMMER NIGHTS

Up over the edge of
the hill climbs the
bloody moon and

now it lifts the far
river to its old familiar
tune and the hazy

dreamlike field—and all
is summer quiet, summer
nights' light airy shadow.

(JUNE)

"BY THE RUDE BRIDGE . . ."

Crazy wheel of days
in the heat, the revolution
spaced to summer's

insistence. That sweat,
the dust, time earlier they
must have walked, run,

all the way from Lexington
to Concord: "By the rude
bridge that arched the flood . . ."

By that enfolding small river
wanders along by grasses'
marge, by thoughtless stones.

(JULY)

VACATION'S END

Opened door chinks
let sun's restlessness

inside eighth month
going down now

earlier as day begins
later, time running down,

air shifts to edge
of summer's end

and here they've gone,
beach emptying

to birds, clouds,
flash of fish, tidal

waters waiting, shifting,
ripple in slight wind.

(AUGUST)

HELEN'S HOUSE

Early morning far trees lift
through mist in faint outline

under sun's first rose,
dawn's opalescence here,

fall's fading rush to color,
chill under the soft air.

Foreground's the planted small fruit trees,
cut lawn, the firs, as now

on tall dying tree beyond
bird suddenly sits on sticklike branch.

Walk off into this weather?
Meld finally in such air?

See goldenrod, marigold, yarrow, tansey
wait for their turn.

(SEPTEMBER)

OLD DAYS

River's old look
from summers ago
we'd come to swim

now yellow, yellow
rustling, flickering
leaves in sun

middle of October
water's up, high sky's blue,
bank's mud's moved,

edge is
closer,
nearer than then.

(OCTOBER)

THE TALLY

Sitting at table
wedged back against wall,

the food goes down in
lumps swallowed

in hunger, in
peculiar friendship

meets rightly again
without reason

more than common bond, the children
or the old cannot reach

for more
for themselves.

We'll wonder,
wander, in November,

count days and ways
to remember, keep away

from the tally,
the accounting.

(NOVEMBER)

MEMORY

I'd wanted
ease of year,
light in the darkness,
end of fears.

For the babe newborn
was my belief,
in the manger,
in that simple barn.

So since childhood
animals
brought back kindness,
made possible care.

But this world now
with its want, its pain,
its tyrannic confusions
and hopelessness,

sees no star
far shining,
no wonder as light
in the night.

Only us then
remember, discover,
still can care for
the human.

(DECEMBER)

Index of Titles